the zen of
watching birds

the zen of
watching birds
wit, wisdom, and inspiration

foreword by Bruce Barcott
edited by Katharine Wroth
illustrations by Kate Quinby

SKIPSTONE

Richard Cannings quote excerpted from *An Enchantment of Birds*, by Richard Cannings, published 2007
by Greystone Books: an imprint of D&M Publishers Inc. Reprinted with permission of the publisher.
Wade Graham quote reprinted by permission from Outside Magazine, © 1998, Mariah Media, Inc.
Jonathan Rosen quote excerpted from *The Life of the Skies: Birding at the End of Nature* (Farrar, Straus,
and Giroux, 2008). Lorna Salzman quote excerpted from the article "Assertiveness Training for Women
Birders," (www.lornasalzman.com)

Published by Skipstone, an imprint of The Mountaineers Books
Manufactured in the United States of America

First printing 2009
12 11 10 09   5 4 3 2 1

Compiled and edited by Katharine Wroth
Illustrations by Kate Quinby
Design by Heidi Smets
Cover photograph © 2009 JupiterImages Corporation

ISBN 978-1-59485-272-5

Library of Congress Cataloging-in-Publication Data
The zen of watching birds : wit, wisdom, and inspiration / foreword by
Bruce Barcott ; edited by Katharine Wroth ; illustrations by Kate Quinby.
     p. cm.
 ISBN-13: 978-1-59485-272-5 (alk. paper)
 1. Bird watching—Quotations, maxims, etc. I. Wroth, Katharine.
 QL677.5.Z46 2009
 598.072'34—dc22
                    2009015071

Skipstone books may be purchased for corporate, educational, or other
promotional sales. For special discounts and information, contact our
Sales Department at 800-553-4453 or mbooks@mountaineersbooks.org.

Skipstone
1001 SW Klickitat Way, Suite 201
Seattle, Washington 98134
206.223.6303
www.skipstonepress.org
www.mountaineersbooks.org

SUSTAINABLE Certified Fiber
FORESTRY Sourcing
INITIATIVE
Label applies to the text stock www.sfiprogram.org

L I V E   L I F E .   M A K E   R I P P L E S .

What would the world be without birds?

—Roger Tory Peterson

keeping watch

by Bruce Barcott

Some places I know by their sound. Some places I know by their scent. But my favorite places are those I know by their birds.

It's a strange kind of sense memory, one that didn't develop until adulthood. I can trace its emergence to a warm summer night about ten years ago when I was camping in the San Juan Islands of Washington. As dusk fell and I snuggled into my sleeping bag, the song of a single bird curled out from the nearby forest. The sound was like nothing I'd ever heard before (though surely I must have): a rising spiral, elegiac and bittersweet. It echoed across an open meadow and curled into my ears. I lay there, not moving, mesmerized. The rustle and clatter of the day slowly fell away until finally the bird performed alone, a featured soloist singing the evening down.

The next morning I asked around. "Anybody else hear that bird last night?" Nobody had.

Later, an experienced birder nodded when I tried to describe the sound. "Must have been a Swainson's thrush. They've got a pretty little song." He said this with the nonchalance of a man describing a bowl of corn flakes.

No, no, I thought. Girls in dresses are pretty. This bird was a revelation, a miracle. What I'd heard was a minimalist *Ode to Joy*. "Pretty" didn't begin to describe it.

Indeed, it was a Swainson's thrush: Common, dullish in appearance, an easily checked box on any American birder's life list. Yet from that moment the thrush became the San Juan Islands in the gallery of my mind. In the years that followed, other birds became other places. The arctic tern, a wheeling, diving, sharp-billed acrobat, became Svalbard, a lonely ice-and-tundra archipelago in the Arctic Ocean. The scarlet macaw became the Belizean jungle. The brown pelican became the coast of Baja, Mexico. The sandhill crane became the corn-stubble fields of Nebraska. The northern flicker became Colorado's Rocky Mountains.

The irony, of course, is that most of those birds are travelers themselves, less connected to the landscape than the terrestrial creatures around them. Yet in my mind the attachment of bird to landscape remains as strong and evocative as ever. I suspect it has something to do with this simple fact: Birds show themselves. Wild mammals generally hide from humans, and for good reason—we tend to kill them. Birds, by contrast, are often spectacularly visible or audible, and sometimes both. They abide the presence of humans with indifference, confident in their ability to elude our grasp.

As I write this I'm outside, enjoying a rare sunny day in late winter in the Pacific Northwest, and an early American robin has alighted on the porch rail, not six feet from my hand. The bird cocks its head and sizes me up. I do the same to him. After drinking in the sight of its copper-pipe breast, a gift of color on a gunmetal day, I notice as if for the first time the white ring around the bird's eye. It's beyond dramatic. It's kabuki makeup. And then, just when I'm getting a good look at it, this hollow-boned descendant of dinosaurs twitches its wings and disappears.

For me the Zen of watching birds is about exactly that—watching birds. It may sound trite, but it's a point that sometimes gets lost in the rush to compile life lists and see the rarest of the rare. I've spent time with hardcore birders. I'm always amazed by their keen eyesight and dedication to the chase. Keeping lists is a fine activity, and I may yet be struck by see-them-all fever. But for now, I'm happy to take each one as it comes. Let the most common sparrow or thrush fire my curiosity. I walk into the landscape with my eyes and ears open to what's soaring and perching and eating and singing all around.

As you read through this collection, you will undoubtedly find something resembling your experience expressed in the words of others. Louis J. Halle's quote sums up my own path: "I never heard a wood thrush until I was a grown man, though I must have been surrounded by them every spring," he once wrote. "Each year I discover new sights and sounds to teach me how blind and deaf I must still be." That sense of awakening is part of the wonder of bird watching. We see a new bird or hear a common song with fresh ears and wonder, *How could I have missed that before?* A wild, mysterious world is out there. We can rush past with narrowed eyes and closed ears or we can stop, look, and listen.

songs that inspire

Whether it's the caw of a crow or the trill of a thrush, the voices of birds make our world— both personal and planetary—come alive.

A bird does not sing because it has an answer. It sings because it has a song.

—Chinese proverb

The note of the white-throated sparrow, a very inspiriting but almost wiry sound, was first heard in the morning, and with this all the woods rang.

—Henry David Thoreau

Spring birdsong! Music to our ears! There's nothing like it to banish the memory of winter's chilly silence and lift our spirits.

—Marie Read

The sound of birds is heaven. It stops the noise in my mind.

—Carly Simon

Always, wherever heard, the song of the oriole suggests
sunshine and a letting-go of winter and sad times.

—Elizabeth Grinnell

With the first hints of spring came the brave little bluebirds, darling singers as blue as the best sky, and of course we all loved them. Their rich, crispy warbling is perfectly delightful, soothing and cheering, sweet and whisperingly low, Nature's fine love touches, every note going straight home into one's heart.

—John Muir

I hear the whispering voice of Spring,
The thrush's trill, the robin's cry,
Like some poor bird with prisoned wing
That sits and sings, but longs to fly.

—Oliver Wendell Holmes

It was on a June afternoon, when the sunbeams slanted lazily through the heavy summer air, tipping the fern fronds, and giving a touch of golden enchantment to the brown leaves that strewed the ground. *Kree-ah, kree-up*, came the sweet, rich call, first from one side and then another, till a dozen thrushes gathered. Then from their leafy covers rose the grave beautiful song. It seemed the choral of a dream, in which each note came forth as an inspiration.

—Florence Merriam Bailey

There's this wonderful Zen parable ... If you listen to the thrush and hear a thrush, you've not really heard the thrush. But if you listen to a thrush and hear a miracle, then you've heard the thrush.

—Donald Kroodsma

When a solitary great Carolina wren came one August day and took up its abode near me and sang and called and warbled as I had heard it long before on the Potomac, how it brought the old days, the old scenes back again, and made me for the moment younger by all those years!

—John Burroughs

In the desert a fountain is springing,
In the wide waste there still is a tree,
And a bird in the solitude singing,
Which speaks to my spirit of thee.

—Lord Byron

Mockingbirds don't do one thing but make music for us to enjoy. They don't eat up people's gardens, don't nest in corncribs, they don't do one thing but sing their hearts out for us. That's why it's a sin to kill a mockingbird.

—Harper Lee

In some notes the nightingale is still a bird; then it rises above its class and seems to suggest to every winged creature what singing is truly like.

—Johann Wolfgang Von Goethe

People who see birds and hear their songs—in spite of the roar of traffic or the bustle of the day—take greater joy in the world around them.

—Peggy Lantz

Sing on, dear bird! thy music unto me
Comes as a dream of days for ever fled.
Sing on, sing on! it calms my aching heart
Thy melody to hear; it bids me know,
There is, there can be, purity on earth.

—Mary Cutts

hatching an interest

They are everywhere around us, these winged
creatures, but the moment we first see them,
hear them, discover their quirks—that is a
moment to remember.

I just love the shape of the birds, and that they are always moving, never still. They're little bundles of mystery to me.

—Amy Ruppel

Birding runs in the blood. If it is there, you'll know fairly quickly, and this often starts at a younger age than you may expect.

—Jessie Barry

When I started birding at six, I didn't know anyone else who was interested. I had no idea of how to go about it. I had no field guide, no binoculars. I became fascinated with birds, any birds, and would scatter breadcrumbs around the lawn and creep up to them to get better looks at the sparrows and Starlings.

—Kenn Kaufman

As a kid in Missouri, I would climb a tree in spring just to view the color of the blue robin eggs in the nest.

—Darren Peterie

It's not hard, once you've got birds to look at, to spark a kid's imagination … Birds have these qualities that we as humans completely admire. They're beautifully colored in many cases, they make amazing noises, and they can do something we've only been able to do in the last 100 years, which is fly.

—Bill Thompson III

I remember feeling enclosed by the dark green of the trees, staring up at the little bird on a branch. I remember that the bird seemed to look back at me, and I felt like the four of us—Jim, Dad, the owl, and me—were the only beings left on Earth. It was an absolutely gorgeous sensation.

—Dan Koeppel

Binoculars and a field guide. One confers supernatural intimacy. The other unlocks the secrets of each bird's identity. You've got flint; you've got steel. The natural inquisitiveness of children is the tinder.

—Pete Dunne

You'd have a lot more trouble trying to get people interested in solitary wasps, or fish, fascinating creatures though they are—because we don't see them, we don't have the affinity to them, and we can't attract them to our backyards. So I think that birds are one of our focal points for getting people attached to nature again, and loving it, and seeing changes, and being concerned. Much more than any other type of nature.

—Don Stokes

A man's interest in a single bluebird is worth more than a complete but dry list of the fauna and flora of a town.

—Henry David Thoreau

Not to have so much as a bowing acquaintance with the birds that nest in our gardens or under the very eaves of our houses; that haunt our wood-piles; keep our fruit-trees free from slugs; waken us with their songs, and enliven our walks along the roadside and through the woods, seems to be, at least, a breach of etiquette toward some of our most kindly disposed neighbors.

—Neltje Blanchan

Birds are the most popular group in the animal kingdom.
We feed them and tame them and think we know them.
And yet they inhabit a world which is really rather
mysterious. Once they take off from our bird tables or our
lawns they disappear into a world of their own.

—Sir David Attenborough

Bird watching was one of the first activities that I encountered where I could totally just lose myself and be in sync with nature.

—Christine Reed

We arrive on this planet unaware of everything except
our physical comfort. As our eyes clear, eventually we
notice a bird. In my case that took longer than for most,
but perhaps living twenty-three years without once seeing
a chickadee made me appreciate the vision all the more
when my eyes finally focused.

—Laura Erickson

Some ladies, beginning the study of birds, once wrote to me, asking if I would not please come and help them, and set them right about certain birds in dispute. I replied that that would be getting their knowledge too easily; that what I and any one else told them they would be very apt to forget, but that the things they found out themselves they would always remember.

—John Burroughs

I never heard even a wood thrush until I was a grown man,
though I must have been surrounded by them every spring.
Each year I discover new sights and sounds to teach me
how blind and deaf I must still be.

—Louis J. Halle

To millions of Americans, the season's first robin means that the grip of winter is broken. Its coming is an event reported in newspapers and told eagerly at the breakfast table.

—Rachel Carson

Sitting at breakfast looking out at a snowscape animated by jays, chickadees, grosbeaks and a nuthatch or two makes me feel regal, as if I were one of those French kings with his own private aviary, gathered from the earth's far corners for my amusement.

—John Cole

If life is, as some hold it to be, a vast melancholy ocean over which ships more or less sorrow-laden continually pass and play, yet there lie here and there upon it isles of consolation on to which we may step out and for a time forget the winds and waves. One of these we may call Bird-isle—the island of watching and being entertained by the habits and humours of birds …

—Edmund Selous

Birdwatching implies on the one hand this stillness, this quiet, this repose, and at the same time an intense alertness, because if you sit in the fields dreaming the undreamt dreams of your short night, all the birds will have gone long before you realize that the sun is warming your back.

—Anthony Bloom

Birds provide people with a deeper connection to nature and to all living things. That's something we all seek and all need … And in this day and age we need it even more, because a lot of modern life involves disconnecting from nature, having stressful lives in which we surround ourselves with technology.

—Lillian Stokes

Prying back a heavy and prickly branch, I stepped inside the skirt of the tree and saw a pair of bright yellow eyes staring at me from the catlike face of a small owl. My heart raced; I did not know what to do. I felt almost giddy to see a creature from my dreams, at eye level, his face less than three feet from my own.

—Paul Bannick

Whatever the origins of this interest, it is indeed an enchantment. Once the spell has been cast, you forever experience the world differently, eyeing forests as if you were a woodpecker looking for nesting snags, subconsciously counting migrating geese as they fly overhead, trying to decide if that hooting owl is a male or female. Although some might think that these habits border on an obsession, I feel that the world would be a better place if we all looked more closely at birds and tried to understand how they perceive their surroundings.

—Richard Cannings

It is as if I, and not just the morning, have now been filled with fresh clear light. To be out-of-doors at sunrise with every sense alert, attuned to the slightest movement, to the cut of every wing. To hear the bird song from the bushes, the woodpecker drumming on a nearby stump—that in itself has been worth something. It has shaken me out of the numbness of my everyday consciousness.

—Candace Savage

a full-fledged obsession

Whatever they call themselves—birders, twitchers, chasers—there's a certain breed of person who simply can't get enough.

Everyone is a birdwatcher, but there are two kinds of birdwatchers: those who know what they are and those who haven't yet realized it.

—Jonathan Rosen

I love birds and it's just the way I'm wired.

—Sharon Stiteler

Watching birds is easy. But *knowing* them is another matter.

—Ted Murin

You become so much interested in the families you are
watching that you feel as if their troubles were yours,
and are haunted by the fear that they will think you have
something to do with their accidents.

—Florence Merriam Bailey

I think birding gets more interesting the more you get into it. It does for me … To avoid falling into a rut of expectations, I challenge myself to really identify some of the birds I see. I'll find a gnatcatcher in New Jersey and try to rule out Black-capped, or study a meadowlark to try to identify it by plumage.

—David Sibley

When you talk to birders, one of the most common themes in why they enjoy birding is because they're always learning something while they're out there. You can bird your entire life and still not know it all and still not have seen it all.

—Julie Brashears

I like to go birding with a question or two in mind … the consistency of the pale supra-loral in Dusky Flycatcher or the call notes of Cassin's Sparrow, for example. Birding with a purpose never becomes boring.

—Will Russell

The observation of birds may be a superstition, a tradition, an art, a science, a pleasure, a hobby, or a bore; this depends entirely on the nature of the observer.

—James Fisher

Five scissor-tailed flycatchers fly from a barbed wire fence and swoop upwards in formation, five rosy breasts arched towards the sun, five impossibly long tails fluttering earthward. The tails flutter like the cloth tails I taped to the kites I flew as a kid.

—Ken Boothroyd

We ardent birders share not only a skill and craft but also a state of mind—more, a state of heart, one akin to love.

—Todd Newberry

[B]irders, as the committed know themselves, will argue that it is in fact a sport of considerable sophistication and sometimes daring risk—a game that requires its best players to be intrepid travelers and skilled naturalists who can identify feathered specks by arcane distinguishing characteristics picked out in leafy darkness, through sheets of rain, or at great distance; who can name an unseen singer by slight variation of pitch discerned from the general chatter of the forest; and who will go to great, sometimes foolish lengths to spy those evanescent and rare birds not yet cited in their life lists—the bird-watcher's equivalent of the gunfighter's notched barrel.

—Wade Graham

Birdwatching is about as entertaining as an obsessive hobby popular with beardy men bearing binoculars can be.

—Carolyn O'Donnell

[As] one fanatical chaser once told me: Anyone can be obsessed with Cameron Diaz. But it takes a real man—or at least a real secure man—to be obsessed with birds.

—Mark Obmascik

I can only describe it as a spiritual, almost religious
dimension, which marks off the true birder from the
person who has only a passing interest.

—Stephen Moss

I can't remember a time from the age of 12 when I haven't been interested in bird watching. It's a way of life for me. I eat, drink and sleep birds. It has become a total fascination.

—Mike Hodgson

It felt weird to return to New York. After the excitements of South Texas, I was hollow and restless, like an addict in withdrawal. It was a chore to make myself comprehensible to friends. I couldn't keep my mind on my work. Every night, I lay down with bird books and read about other trips I could take, studied the field markings of species I hadn't seen, and then dreamed vividly of birds.

—Jonathan Franzen

Just this morning … I saw a mourning warbler that was probably hatched in a spruce bog in Quebec, a prairie warbler on its way to Jamaica or Hispaniola, and a red-eyed vireo that will winter in the Amazon basin. Tomorrow they'll be gone, and a whole new cast of migrants will have arrived overnight. Every time I step off the back porch, it's a new adventure.

— Scott Weidensaul

Who else but a birder can separate prothonotary from other forms of yellow? We recognize that shade only because we know the bird and its name.

—Jack Connor

We enjoy seeing uncommon birds, but we also enjoy seeing common birds doing uncommon things.

—John and Gloria Tveten

The general dangers presented to all birders are always with us: ticks, snakes, chiggers, mosquitoes, jaguars, Montezuma's Revenge and rental car breakdowns, though these are not found necessarily in the same place at the same time.

—Lorna Salzman

Birding is the best and most exciting pursuit in the world, a glorified never-ending one. And the whole experience of a foreign trip, whether you see 10 new birds or 500, is simply too good to miss.

—Phoebe Snetsinger

My style is definitely sitting and watching. Someone might organize a bird walk and ask me to lead it for one or two miles. Well, two hours might go by and we'd only be a quarter of a mile from where we started and have to turn around and go back to the car. I'm convinced that I see just as many birds as people who spend their time hiking. And by spending less time walking, I have more time for lifting my binoculars and looking at birds.

—David Sibley

Every step I take falls in the footsteps of birders who
came before. Every time I raise binoculars, there are two
sets of hands bringing the instruments to bear—one
flesh and blood, one woven of the shadows cast by
those ornithological giants who came before and whose
knowledge is my hereditary foundation.

—Pete Dunne

At its best, in its heightened moments, birdwatching can encourage a state of being close to rapture—the forgetfulness that blends the individual consciousness with something other than itself.

—Graeme Gibson

Most birds live at a level of intensity that we can't match. Watching a bird I'm often reminded of just what an intense experience life can be.

—Kenn Kaufman

nesting instincts

At a glance, one might not think humans and birds
have much in common. But don't let the wings
and feathers mislead you: similarities abound.

In our mother's womb we float in water, a remnant of our aquatic origins that we somehow took with us when we left the oceans that spawned us eons ago. But where are the woods, the fertile forests that also constituted the womb of our species? Birds bring us fragments, not in their beaks, but on their backs.

—Jonathan Rosen

I'm youth, I'm joy, I'm a little bird that has broken out of the egg.

—James M. Barrie

O birds, your perfect virtues bring,
Your song, your forms, your rhythmic flight,
Your manners for your heart's delight,
Nestle in hedge, or barn, or roof,
Here weave your chamber weather-proof,
Forgive our harms, and condescend
To man, as to a lubber friend,
And, generous, teach his awkward race
Courage, and probity, and grace!

—Ralph Waldo Emerson

I never wanted to weigh more heavily on a man than a bird.

—Coco Chanel, on why she never married her lovers

I think we're a kind of desperation. We're sort of a maddening luxury. The basic and essential human is the woman, and all that we're doing is trying to brighten up the place. That's why all the birds who belong to our sex have prettier feathers—because males have got to try and justify their existence.

—Orson Welles

You may call a jay a bird. Well, so he is, in a measure—
because he's got feathers on him, and don't belong to
no church, perhaps; but otherwise he is just as much
a human as you be. And I'll tell you for why. A jay's
gifts and instincts, and feelings, and interests, cover the
whole ground. A jay hasn't got any more principle than a
Congressman.

—Mark Twain

His imagination resembled the wings of an ostrich. It enabled him to run, though not to soar.

—Thomas Babington Macaulay

If you keep your feathers well oiled the water of criticism will run off as from a duck's back.

—Ellen Henrietta Swallow Richards

[To] a poet, the human community is like the community of birds to a bird, singing to each other. Love is one of the reasons we are singing to one another, love of language itself, love of sound, love of singing itself, and love of the other birds.

—Sharon Olds

Our work is the same as the House People's—scratching and hopping about all day, to fill the stomachs of ourselves and families, and try to make them contented ... Of course we have the advantage over you in the matter of clothes, for as ours grow on, we are never bothered with shopping, and are always sure of a good fit.

—Mabel Osgood Wright

"Hope" is the thing with feathers—
That perches in the soul—
And sings the tunes without the words—
And never stops—at all—

—Emily Dickinson

My heart is like a singing bird.

—Christina Rossetti

I'd been told that it was bad to anthropomorphize,
but I could no longer remember why. It was, in any
case, anthropomorphic only to see yourself in other
species, not to see them in yourself. To be hungry all
the time, to be mad for sex, to not believe in global
warming, to be shortsighted, to live without thought of
your grandchildren, to spend half your life on personal
grooming, to be perpetually on guard, to be compulsive,
to be habit-bound, to be avid, to be unimpressed with
humanity, to prefer your own kind: these were all ways of
being like a bird.

—Jonathan Franzen

Birds possess a power that seems superhuman—the way they soar through the sky. But what makes them most fascinating to people are their more human qualities: how they migrate and nest and raise families and even sing.

—Dan Koeppel

You are the gull, Jo, strong and wild, fond of the storm and the wind, flying far out to sea, and happy all alone. Meg is the turtle-dove, and Amy is like the lark she writes about, trying to get up among the clouds, but always dropping down into its nest again.

—Louisa May Alcott

Humans, whatever their spiritual pursuits, are just animals, after all, and what better way to understand human existence than to study birds?

—Peter Pyle

dreams of flight

Flying: the avian skill that humans most admire
(the worm-eating, somehow not such a draw).
As they soar, we watch, we learn, we imagine
ourselves in their place.

The shell must break before the bird can fly.

—Alfred Lord Tennyson

Birds are the life of the skies, and when they fly, they reveal the thoughts of the skies.

—D. H. Lawrence

There are birds whose flight predicts a storm; but there are also birds whose flight predicts a calm.

—George Matheson

There are mountaintops so high and so steep that man has never succeeded in climbing them. But the birds may use them as resting places and soar about in the sky far above them.

—Frank M. Chapman

No bird soars too high, if he soars with his own wings.

—William Blake

Let's say you have a dream that you're a bird flying in the sky, looking down on the earth. Are you quite sure, after you awake, that you dreamed you were a bird? Could you, perhaps, be a bird dreaming you are a person?

—Joan Budilovsky and Eve Adamson

Oh that I had wings like a dove!

—Psalm 55:6

I wish I had wings, she thought. *Everything would be easier if we had wings.*

—Lois Lowry

I would like to fly out of my head,
but that is out of the question.

—Anne Sexton

I live in company with a body, a silent companion, exacting and eternal. He it is who notes that individuality which is the seal of the weakness of our race. My soul has wings, but the brutal jailer is strict.

—Eugène Delacroix

I believe that if one always looked at the skies, one would end up with wings.

—Gustave Flaubert

The girls lifted their faces to watch the flight of a crow beating its way along with strong, vibrant wings, and something in keen sympathy with the bird's wings responded in their own young hearts.

—Frances Bennett Callaway

I sometimes think that the desire to fly after the fashion of birds is an ideal handed down to us by our ancestors who, in their grueling travels across trackless lands in prehistoric times, looked enviously on the birds soaring freely through space, at full speed, above all obstacles, on the infinite highway of the air.

—Wilbur Wright

If I had to choose, I would rather have birds than airplanes.

—Charles Lindbergh

I will not change my horse with any that treads but on four pasterns …. When I bestride him, I soar, I am a hawk; he trots the air.

—Shakespeare *(Henry V)*

[Y]ou will feel strong, glad, firm, high, proud, successful, satisfied, powerful, and elevated—as though you had conquered life and had a high purpose.

—E. B. White

When the flight is not high the fall is not heavy.

—Chinese proverb

Some researchers believe that in our dreams we go back to preborn states, make contact with the state of birds, and realize our innate ability to fly.

—Klaus Vollmar

I fly in dreams, I know it is my privilege, I do not recall
a single situation in dreams when I was unable to fly. To
execute every sort of curve and angle with a light impulse,
a flying mathematics—that is so distinct a happiness that it
has permanently suffused my basic sense of happiness.

—Friedrich Nietzsche

[T]o lose the chance to see frigate-birds soaring in circles above the storm, or a file of pelicans winging their way homeward across the crimson afterglow of the sunset, or a myriad of terns flashing in the bright light of midday as they hover in a shifting maze above the beach—why, the loss is like the loss of a gallery of the masterpieces of the artists of old time.

—Theodore Roosevelt

I hope you love birds too. It is economical. It saves going to heaven.

—Emily Dickinson